War Fever

British Anarchism Succumbs to War Fever

Published by Active Distribution, 2023

ISBN 978-1-914567-36-0

www.activedistribution.org

Preface

British Anarchism Succumbs to War Fever

In February 2022, the Russian Armed Forces invaded Ukrainian territory, beginning an occupation and open warfare. This followed eight years of smouldering conflict between the Ukrainian state and Russian-backed separatists in the Donbas region of Ukraine, and the annexation of Crimea. Some anarchists, antifascists, and other anti-authoritarians in Ukraine decided to participate in the armed forces of the state to combat the Russian invasion. This was an organised, collective project with a political manifesto, under the banner of 'The Resistance Committee' and 'Operation Solidarity'.

Many anarchists in Britain responded with uncritical support for the project and began actively aiding the Ukrainian war effort, raising funds for military supplies and spreading war propaganda. A minority of anarchists, on the other hand, raised the banner of "no war but the class war", opposing war itself while advocating for working class internationalism, against all factions of the ruling class. This latter position, previously an uncontroversial expression of anarchist-communist politics, was all of a sudden anathema.

Notable anarchist papers in Britain such as Freedom and Organise! made the case for supporting the war effort and denounced those who would disagree. They did so, in my view, by comprehensively dismantling or distorting basic anarchist ideas. It was primarily in response to these articles that I wrote my critique, but it was clear that the point of view they set out was fiercely held by people across the anarchist milieu. The intention, then, was not to tell Ukrainian anarchists what they should be doing, but rather, in the context of debate among anarchists in Britain, to defend a theory and practice of anarchism that is revolutionary, internationalist, and anti-militarist.

I make this argument not for the sake of "ideological purity", in callous disregard for those suffering and dying, but because I think that revolutionary anarchism (as I understand it) offers the best way to fight against states, capitalism, and the wars they produce, and to change society in doing so. It is with the greatest compassion for the victims that I wish to see the war brought quickly to an end. The question is how can we oppose war without simply reproducing the conditions that generate it, or for that matter intensifying and generalising it. The essential step is to break with the logic of nationalism, militarism, and state politics in general.

This is not a question of neutrality, which it might appear from the perspective of nation versus nation. To be neutral in a situation of oppression is to side with the oppressor, our critics would rightly reply. Rather, we revolutionary anarchists are partisans of the oppressed and exploited people in every nation. We are against domination in all its forms, and will not collaborate with one oppressor to fight another. Our "side" is the global working class, against those who exploit and control our lives, and ultimately take them from us.

We have entered an age of unending and manifold crisis, producing a general increase of authoritarian nationalism, rising imperialist tensions, and consequent war. Anarchists must have the theoretical grounding and practical strategies to continue the struggle towards anarchy in such conditions. Therefore, anarchism can't be reserved as a luxury for liberal democratic nations in peace-time and treated as a dogmatic irrelevance everywhere else. If anarchists abandon anti-militarism and internationalism at this crucial moment, not only will we be marching in step with our masters towards the graveyard of imperialist conflagration, we will also be closing off any paths towards freedom.

Alex Alder
22nd October 2023

British Anarchism Succumbs to War Fever

Alex Alder

2nd February 2023

Everyone is against war in the abstract – even the arms industry executives can tell themselves that they are merely providing for defence and global order, deterring war in doing so. But when war breaks out the sentiment is made irrelevant. Peace-loving or not, war is here, and you are either with your nation, your people, or against them. Peace will come with victory. In any case, your side is the righteous cause, because you fight for freedom and justice, for democracy and stability, because your enemy were the aggressors, and tyrants and devils to boot. The bloodshed is so easily sanctified.

Anarchism cuts right through such mystification. We say it as we see it: the workers of different nations are sent to slaughter each other in the interests of their rulers. Anti-militarism is a core principle of anarchism. We understand armies to be a violent force underwriting political authority (or those who would conquer it). We point to the role of military force in suppressing uprisings and strikes at home, while imposing national interests, enforcing capitalist markets, and ruling colonies abroad. Military research and production is a highly profitable investment of private capital and public funds, not least as a subsidised source of technological development (for the purposes of social control and generating profit). We consider how the military system of strict hierarchy and discipline, alongside its culture of chauvinism and othering,[1] breaks down the human character and reshapes it to the needs of those in command.

---

1. Anarchists are no less susceptible to these pressures, for all our ideals, as can be seen with anarchist fighters in Ukraine referring to Russian soldiers as 'orcs' and 'Putin's horde'.

So how is it that today the anarchist movement in Britain (and elsewhere) is supporting one nation's military against another, ideologically justifying and materially provisioning[2] the Ukrainian war effort? Are we seeing something altogether new that would lead us to question and revise our principles? No, we are facing the same old tragedy. Our anti-militarist, internationalist, and revolutionary perspective is as vital as ever. At this present stage, the struggle for liberation is caught in the no-man's-land between imperialist invasion on the one side, and national defence (backed by an opposing imperialism) on the other. To seek purpose in either trench would be just more fuel in the furnace of capitalist warfare; it would mean allegiance to the state against anarchy.

---

2. Anarchists have been raising funds for the 'Solidarity Collectives' (formerly 'Operation Solidarity) who provide military supplies to libertarian and antifascist activists in the Ukrainian Armed Forces (in addition to humanitarian aid). Between February and June 2022, out of €59,680 spent by Operation Solidarity, €41,404 was used for 'military causes". https://operation-solidarity.org/2022/07/06/operation-solidarity-the-end/

National Defence and Anti-Imperialism

From the long-standing anarchist paper *Freedom* and anarcho-communist Anarchist Federation (AFed), to the anarchist "scene" around antifascist and other activist groups, war fever is rife. At first this involved cheerleading for the 'Anti-authoritarian Platoon', a unit of the Territorial Defence made up of anarchists and antifascists, among others.[3] Participation in military structures was explained by the need to defend themselves, and softened by a narrative of independent popular resistance. But the reality was quite different. The Territorial Defence Forces are the reserve force of the Ukrainian military, subject to its command structure. There is no question of autonomy. A member of the Anti-authoritarian Platoon observed that in their unit "there [was] normal military hierarchy with section commanders and

---

3. Since the beginning of the war, they have dispersed into various Territorial Defence and regular army units (many of them transferring so as to be closer to the frontline), but still connected through the Resistance Committee and supported by the Solidarity Collectives.

platoon commander subordinate to higher military officers."[4] Other anarchists and antifascists joined the regular army. Rhetoric aside, this means collaboration in the national defence by joining the state military, one way or another.

That some people choose to join or support the military defence of the nation in which they reside when threatened by imperialist domination is understandable[5] and I do not judge anyone making such difficult choices. But it is not anarchism – it is not compatible with anarchist ideas or practices. No one lives up to their ideals in everything they do, but these compromises and contradictions should be accepted as such, not assimilated into our theory and practice such that in turn our movement is assimilated into the society of capital and state.

---

4. ' 'Defensive war as an act of popular resistance...'': Exclusive Interview with an Anarchist Fighter of the Territorial Defense Forces of Ukraine', *Militant Wire*.
5. Just as it is understandable that other people will seek to escape the war-zones and seek refuge elsewhere, to evade being drafted, or desert from the military.

As the reality of collaboration became clearer to anarchists in Britain, the message widened to support for the defence of Ukraine, maintaining the rhetoric of 'popular resistance'. "From Ukraine to Scotland to Western Sahara to Palestine to Tatarstan, we stand with the people resisting imperialism,"[6] proclaims Darya Rustamova in the pages of *Freedom* (and reprinted by AFed). This statement raises more questions than it answers. Who are "the people"? By what means are they resisting? To what end? In the past, AFed were able to see through such empty talk, arguing that "As anarchist communists, we have always opposed nationalism, and have always marked our distance from the left through vocally opposing all nationalism — including that of 'oppressed nations'. While we oppose oppression, exploitation and dispossession on national grounds, and oppose imperialism and imperialist warfare, we refuse to fall into the trap so common on the left of identifying with the underdog side and glorifying 'the

6. 'A thousand red flags', Darya Rustamova. *Freedom*.

resistance' — however 'critically' — which is readily observable within Leninist/Trotskyist circles."[7]

Rustamova's article, *A Thousand Red Flags*, makes explicit their nationalist premises with a typically leftist differentiation between good and bad nationalism. The nuance between different expressions of nationalism in different contexts is no doubt real and significant. The nationalism of a colony struggling for independence is obviously different from the nationalism of the empire. Yet, for both the state is their end (to establish, defend, or expand); both suppress or obscure the class divide and other hierarchies beneath nationality; and both serve the interests of a ruling class ('native' or 'foreign'). The common features of all nationalisms that define them as such are precisely those we reject as anarchists and revolutionary internationalists.

"Anarchists have taken to defence of their homeland,"[8] announced the editor of AFed's magazine,

---

7. 'Against Nationalism', Anarchist Federation.
8. 'Editorial', *Organise!* #96.

Organise!, in issue #96. What homeland do anarchists have? The 'homeland' is a sentimental notion of the nation-state in which a person is born. It is the feelings of belonging, allegiance, and nostalgia that bonds the individual to the nation. This clarifies the unquestioned leap that has been made between Ukraine, as a sovereign nation, defending its territory against invasion (i.e. national defence), and anarchists or other individuals defending themselves (i.e. self-defence). It is a powerful argument for going off to fight in so far as few would renounce the right of self-defence. But it assumes identity between the nation and oneself, an identity that anarchists reject. In this way, anarchists went from championing "semi-autonomous" anarchist units in a "popular resistance" to beating the drums of war for the military victory of the Ukrainian state.

The state's ultimate self-justification is preserving the safety and wellbeing of its subjects. War with other nations is, initially, at least, its greatest unifying force. The Ukrainian anarchist magazine

Assembly confirm that "we should understand that the national unity of Ukrainians around Zelensky's power rests only on fear of an external threat".[9] To participate in this unification and justify it with that same instinct of self-preservation is to not only give legitimacy to the state's authority, but also to support its material reinforcement. To assert the necessity of participating in national defence and joining the state military is to accept the necessity of the state. *Assembly* lament that 'the majority of those who identify themselves as anarchists in Ukraine [...] immediately merged with the ruling class in a single nationalist impulse."[10] The state's power over life and death, war and peace, is one of its defining aspects – it is for anarchists to criticise and subvert, not fall back on as a necessary evil.

Alongside the theoretical rejection of national unity, we must question the assumption that our personal safety is tied in with national security.

9. 'War in Ukraine and desertion: Interview with the anarchist group "Assembly" of Kharkiv', International Relations Commission of the Italian Anarchist Federation.
10. *Ibid.*

Thoughts on this are offered by Saša Kaluža, an anarchist in Ukraine, who says that "The goal of the Ukrainian state and their military structures in this war is to keep their power, the goal of the Russian state and their military structures is to seize power. The participation of anarchists in the structures of either of these states does not make the situation any easier for the people living in Ukraine, who are suffering from the war between two states. All the words about the army defending people, society and their land are only part of state propaganda, and history shows this. It is only possible to stop the war by opposing both states."[11] Regarding the volunteer units specifically, they argue that the "Territorial Defence is a good and telling example of how volunteer structures initiated and controlled by the state can only perform volunteer support functions within the state, by state methods and only to protect the state itself, and cannot actually help the population with security and other

11. 'Anarchist Organization in Times of War and Crisis', Saša Kaluža.

primary needs that arise in crisis situations."[12] It can further be doubted that the participation of a hundred or so anarchists and antifascists in the armed forces has any impact on the outcome of the war, whereas as many dedicated agitators could be a significant nucleus of the struggle against war and government itself.[13]

We need to look beyond the black-and-white binary of aggressor and resistance, imperialist and oppressed nations, revealing the complexity of class antagonisms, power structures, and social hierarchies within each nation-state, identifying the latent force of working class internationalism.

In supporting Ukraine, anarchists in Britain have found themselves on the side of NATO, an

---

12. *Ibid.*
13. Back in 2018, in relation to the war against Russian-backed separatists in the Donbass region, but before the full Russian invasion of 2022, Ukrainian anarchist group 'RevDia' (who now participate in the Resistance Committee) argued that "The army is a hierarchical structure, where an ordinary soldier can not influence the course of the war", and that "...the army does not protect us. And does not defend our interests". Quoting 'Thought of war' and 'Anarchism in Action', RevDia.

imperialist military alliance that defends the interests of the core capitalist nations in Europe and North America. But rather than take this as an opportunity to repudiate NATO they have wavered in their opposition, sympathising with Western imperialism as a check on Russian imperialism. This is most evident in Zosia Brom's article, *'Fuck Leftist Westplaining'*,[14] published in *Freedom* (of which she was an editor at the time), and reprinted in *Organise!* #96 by AFed. Supposing the necessity of NATO membership for the security of Eastern Europe is no doubt correct from the perspective of state diplomacy and international relations, but we are not politicians and we are not part of the decision making apparatus of the state. As anarchists we must respond to the manoeuvrings of nation-states and imperialist blocs from a working class perspective. Autonomous of all state machinery, its realpolitik is not for us to take up. Our anti-imperialism cannot be the Stalinist reflex of supporting anyone opposed to "the West" – but neither can it involve

14. 'Fuck Leftist Westplaining', Zosia Brom, *Freedom*.

turning to NATO imperialism to defend our rights and safety. Rather than thinking in terms of national agency, we need to be thinking along class lines, in terms of social struggle.

Antifascism and Class Struggle

Neither the Russian nor Ukrainian state can be accurately described as fascist, although both have tolerated, enabled, and utilised fascist elements whenever expedient. However, the Russian state has reached a level of authoritarian nationalism, internal repression, and revanchist expansionism comparable to the fascist regimes of the twentieth century. The Ukrainian state can better be described as a neoliberal, corrupt democracy.[15] It is necessary to thoroughly reject Russian propaganda of "de-nazifying" Ukraine. But anarchists have simply turned this around, framing Ukraine's military defence as an antifascist struggle. This risks legitimising war in the name of antifascism, an ideological manoeuvre

---

15. Although the extra-parliamentary far-right in Ukraine should not be brushed under the rug.

that Putin has so transparently played on. Projecting our antifascist politics onto the national defence of Ukraine does not alter its material reality.

Ideological antifascism can serve to obscure class interests and subordinate revolutionary struggle to popular fronts in defence of the democratic state.[16] The movement towards anarchy is deferred to a future, more opportune time as the immediate threat of fascism redraws the board. The intermediate goal of defending the limited rights of democratic society becomes the only legitimate reference point. Ideological unification is mirrored by social unification in cross-class alliances that bring together ruler and ruled, exploiter and exploited against the exceptional threat.

If it means the defeat of fascism, the shielding of actual life and liberties, conceding one's principles may be understandable. But we should have learned from the twentieth century that it

---

16. This is not a criticism of antifascism in the general sense, but of a particular antifascist ideology that was prevalent in the popular fronts of the mid-twentieth century, and which continues to be present in liberal opposition to fascism.

is nothing but a travesty.[17] Again and again, the democratic state which popular fronts defended gave way to fascism with little more than a whimper. Those states prioritised – through counter-revolution – the consolidation of their authority, even if that meant enabling or embracing fascism. "The fight for a democratic state is inevitably a fight to consolidate the state, and far from crippling totalitarianism, such a fight increases totalitarianism's stranglehold on society."[18] The state can develop towards democracy or dictatorship depending on what is necessary for its continuation. It is through the struggle against the state as such that we can both confront authoritarian tendencies in the intermediate term

---

17. "For revolutionaries, and particularly for anarchists, the tragic experience of Spain in '36 should suffice to keep oneself free of illusions in respect to antifascism, which is no more than the defense of the democratic forms of capitalist management, reconciliation between classes, the option of the 'lesser evil" and the abandonment of the revolutionary horizon." Quoting 'Reflections on the ongoing capitalist butchery', Vamos Hacia La Vida.
18. 'When Insurrections Die', Gilles Dauve.

while overturning the conditions that produce them in the long term.

War and Revolutionary Struggle

Those anarchists supporting Ukraine have revealed a great deal of confusion about how we relate to war as anarchists. Some keep up their anti-war rhetoric while supporting one side against another. Others conflate warfare with the struggle for freedom. And some fully embrace war-mongering, all things being justified by opposition to Russia.

Peter Ó Máille (editor of *Organise!* magazine) off-handedly dispenses with working class anti-militarism in musing that 'For the Anarchist there is only one war which matters and that is the class war, except for when it isn't. There are fascists that need fighting, there are despots, tyrants, and empires. They aren't going to go home due to your strongly worded petition.'[19] We can surely agree on the need to fight against tyrants such as Putin, but the heart of the matter is the means by which we do so. And

19. 'Editorial', *Organise!* #96.

here we find misrepresentation and confusion. War between nations and "class war" are distinct in kind. Anarchists are against war in the sense of military conflict undertaken by political authority. "Class war" is a figurative term, referring to the struggle between classes that is framed by capitalist social relations. Revolutionary class struggle is the collective effort of the working class to transform those social relations, which cannot be altered by war in the proper sense. War, in fact, consecrates them in blood.

The war has been treated, in general, not as a war between two states, but as a struggle for the freedom of Eastern Europe.[20] Russia's victory would reinforce its totalitarian regime internally and encourage the further subjugation of its neighbours, while Russia's defeat, we are told, would incite the collapse of Putin's government and reinforce democratic governance in the region, maintaining favourable conditions for social struggle. Here it is clear that the methods and principles of anarchism

---

20. See, for example, 'Why Do Anarchists Go To War?', by RevDia, March 2022. Featured in *Organise! #96*.

have been entirely discarded in favour of the doctrine of military humanitarianism (exemplified by NATO interventions across the Global South and the Balkans). With such a logic adopted, it was only a matter of time before anarchists started arguing for NATO member nations to send more military aid to Ukraine (or bemoaning the hesitant lack of it).

The political, social, and economic outcomes of war are unpredictable. It is not unlikely that Ukraine will emerge from the war as an authoritarian state, an active partner in NATO's military imperialism, and highly susceptible to far-right ideologies whose zealots will have been empowered by the war in more ways than one. Even if liberal democracy survives in Ukraine, there is no guarantee that these conditions will be favourable to the struggle for liberation. A democratic state commanding popular support will have the free reign to quietly suppress post-war rebellions and quell industrial unrest. Anarchist malcontents will easily be framed as Russian-backed separatists and saboteurs, or simply ignored in the wave of overwhelming patriotism and desire for a return to normality and stability, which could follow a military victory. Either way it is pure speculation, and not a strong basis for the working class to sacrifice itself to the war effort.

Anarchists have always understood that the social transformation we wish to see cannot come about by means of the state or military force of any kind, but must develop from the bottom-up among the oppressed and exploited people themselves. Wars can only impose a new form of authority, even if that new authority is a lesser evil. Deferring the struggle against capitalism and the state until after a "victorious" war only ensures the conditions for further war and oppression remain, while undermining the struggle against them. *War is not a means of liberation.* Just as we use direct action, self-organisation, mutual aid, and sabotage to pursue our revolutionary ends, those same means can be used to undermine tyrants and invaders, without facilitating other forms of domination.

Action From Principle

The coherency of means and ends is a notion fundamental to anarchism. The principles that guide us, and the methods we employ, are a continuous thread linking our partial struggles today with the social revolution we seek to hasten and the free society born thereof. Action from principle underpins everything we do. In defending a course of statist military action, anarchists will have stumbled into basic contradictions. This has been resolved through a series of falsifications and concessions.

Anti-militarism, internationalism, and so on, are all very nice in theory, we are told, but ultimately empty abstractions.[21] They are simply not applicable to the reality faced by anarchists on the ground. This is a separation of theory and practice. Theory belongs in books, we would be led to believe, while

---

21. For example, "The [internationalist] analysis is [...] full of abstractions and unreal at ground level, from where Ukrainian anarchists are asking for our practical help including military equipment". Quoting 'Ukraine – Anarchist Approaches' in *Organise!* #96.

the plans and practices of anarchists are driven by force of circumstances. The lesser evil displaces any self-determined goal as the point of reference, while expediency becomes the measure of all choice. Necessity justifies all, in the end.

What is forgotten is that the theory and practice of anarchism are drawn from one another in a constant process of mutual development. It is from experience – of success and defeat, war and peace, revolution and reaction – from generation to generation, all over the world, that we have cultivated a method of freedom: anarchism. It is false to contrast principles with pragmatism, because our principles are the crystallisation of precisely *what works*.[22] There may be more appealing options in the short term, in relation to more immediate interests, but these will lead us away from our goals. Anarchists, for example, refuse to act within state structures or collaborate with state forces not in obedience to unquestionable dogma, but because we know that by such means we will only perpetuate state power,

22. 'Pragmatism as Ideology', Joseph Kay.

that our struggle will be recuperated into political channels and reshaped by institutional pressures. We know this both through abstract analysis of the modern state, and through the experiences of individuals, organisations, and whole movements.

Such an understanding used to be at the core of the Anarchist Federation. Now they openly disparage anarchist principles as "slogans" used to side-step critical analysis, provoke emotional responses, and shut down debate. Anti-militarist agitation is compared to the manipulative and authoritarian practices of Brexiteers and the far-right.[23] This simply does not reflect the reality of the propaganda work of "No War but the Class War" groups, for whom this slogan is just a masthead.[24] Meanwhile, the editor of their theoretical journal *Organise!* now asserts that "I doubt the theory works past the first barrage of artillery on the neighbourhood."[25]

---

23. 'The Trouble With Slogans', Emma Hayes, *Organise!* #96.
24. See NWBCW Liverpool's list of internationalist positions. https://nwbcwliverpool.wordpress.com/internationalist-positions/
25. 'Editorial', *Organise!* #96.

In that case, we may as well give it up and don our khakis. Anarchism, we would conclude, is nothing but naive idealism, belonging to a more peaceful world than our own. I would say, quite the opposite, that it is precisely in such times of heightened conflict, of raised stakes and mortal threats, that learning from our past is more vital than ever. And I would say, far from limiting ourselves to ideal conditions, the anarchist movement has a strong tradition of anti-militarism in times of war, as well as heroic, constructive efforts in the depths of crisis and disaster.

Once we separate our methods from our goals, our ideas from our actions, we are left only with the rule of expediency: the most efficient means of attaining immediate objectives, regardless of other considerations. If the military victory of Ukraine and collapse of Putin's government comes before all else then there are much more effective ways to pursue this goal than forming ideologically bound "anti-authoritarian" Territorial Defence units made up of volunteers with little to no combat experience. It is entirely logical that anarchists and other left-wing activists fighting in the war would become frustrated with the auxiliary role and bureaucratic limitations faced in the 'Anti-authoritarian Platoon' and disperse into more effective fighting units of the army closer to the frontline. And since "fascists are much better organized in the ranks of the Ukrainian army"[26] – also sharing the motivation to be fighting on the frontline – it is predictable that "attempts to get a place in the military ranks brought [anti-authoritarian fighters] directly to units directly connected with Ukrainian fascist groups"[27] and "in one way or another, becoming forces that support the development of far-right politics in Ukraine".[28] This is the logical outcome of relinquishing anarchist principles to the practical needs of the war effort.

---

26. 'A political and personal statement as well as a review of our solidarity work around the war in Ukraine so far', Anarchist Black Cross Dresden.
27. *Ibid.*
28. *Ibid.*

In our own context, the war fever that has overcome anarchists in Britain will likely lead to support for British military intervention (through military aid and technical support, if not actual combat involvement) and, by extension, NATO imperialism. It is through such means that Ukraine will be able to defeat Russia. Given that NATO members are currently hesitant to escalate into direct conflict between nuclear powers, some anarchists find themselves in the absurd position of being more eager for the generalisation of imperialist war than their own ruling classes. Will anarchists be signing up to the British Army to go kill Russians? We don't have any anarchist MPs to vote for war credits, at least.

The Lesser Evil

In our proletarian condition of dispossession, disempowerment, and alienation, our entire lives have been reduced to a search for the lesser evil. Looking at Russia's brutal invasion of Ukraine, the war crimes it has perpetrated, and the harsh repression brought upon its own citizens, we could identify Ukraine's national defence as the lesser evil. Yet, acknowledging that *there is* a lesser evil does not mean, without further reason, that we should be supporting it. And, from an anarchist perspective, we can find no good reason to collaborate with either state. At the same time, refusing to support one state against another does not mean equating both sides. We don't say that both sides are the same, simply that neither have anything to offer the working class.[29]

The lesser evil is still an evil. In defending its territory, the Ukrainian state has not been transformed into a force for good. While the war rages, the capitalist class in Ukraine has only intensified its exploitation and abuse of the working people, backed by new restrictions on industrial action

---

29. 'Nationalism can offer nothing except further rounds of conflict, which look set to increase in number and severity as national competition over the world's dwindling energy resources increases. When conflict is framed in national terms — understood as the conflict between an oppressed and an oppressor nation — the working class necessarily loses out.' Quoting 'Against Nationalism', Anarchist Federation.

and the dismantling of workers' rights.[30] That is, for those who have not been conscripted to the killing fields. Conscription is a form of slavery, to be resisted at all costs. Ukraine's borders have been closed to all men of conscription age (a category in which trans women have been included, erasing their identity) to enable the rounding up of cannon fodder. Meanwhile, Ukraine contributes to the genocidal war in Tigray, providing support for the use of drones by the Ethiopian military.[31] Along the road of the lesser evil, the political and economic conditions that produce war and dictatorship will continue to perpetuate themselves; 'it is forgotten that to choose an evil

---

30. 'Ukraine's anti-worker law comes into effect', openDemocracy. https://www.opendemocracy.net/en/odr/ukraine-labour-law-wrecks-workers-rights/

31. "Turkey, a member of NATO, sells to the Ethiopian government drones whose engines are manufactured in Ukraine, in Kyiv. The government of Ukraine which – although itself under the threat of imperialism – did not hesitate to provide after-sales service and to send mercenary technicians to teach the Ethiopian imperialist army how to use these drones against the populations in Tigray." http://cnt-ait.info/2022/02/27/tigre-ukraine/

- even if it is a lesser evil - is the best way to pro-
long it."[32]

We need to choose our own battles. The threat
of co-optation and counter-insurgency is that
we seem to be constantly denied the possibility
of fighting on our own terms. Whether that be
pushing social movements into the electoral graveyard, or driving rebellion into the field of military
conflict, our real social strength is lost leaving us
a controlled opposition or a symmetric enemy of
the state that can be isolated and crushed. The
strength of anarchism – what has made it a truly
subversive force outside of and against every system of authority – is that anarchists have constantly struggled to fight on our own terms, to think
and act beyond the choices given to us. If at first
we speak alone with the voice of revolutionary internationalism, the tide can quickly turn – a tide
that not uncommonly surges towards the tail end
and aftermath of war.

---

32. 'The Lesser Evil', Dominique Misein.

Neither East Nor West

Many of the anarchists in Ukraine, and across Eastern Europe, have thrown themselves behind Ukraine's war effort. This creates a tension with anti-militarist, internationalist agitation in Britain and across the world. As Peter Ó Máille puts it, "You just can't bear to listen to Eastern European Anarchists eh? [...You] forget to listen to the fucking locals as [you] act like the Politburo of Anarchism. Please kindly, shut the fuck up."[33] Meanwhile, Zosia Brom bemoans "westplaining" – western leftists condescendingly explaining to Eastern Europeans their own reality. We should "be informed that many Eastern Europe leftists are on the same page here, and we have been discussing it for a while now".[34]

In this way, the debate between anti-militarist anarchists and anarchists supporting the war effort is reframed into a confrontation between Western Europe and Eastern Europe, between Westerners' ignorance and arrogance on the one hand, and the

33. 'Editorial', *Organise!* #96.
34. 'Fuck Leftist Westplaining', Zosia Brom, *Freedom*.

pro-Ukraine "consensus" in Eastern Europe on the other. This is of course a rhetorical device for shaming any criticism. In reality, many anarchists in Eastern Europe, including some in Ukraine itself, have responded to the Russian invasion with internationalist, anti-militarist propaganda and action. The anarchist collective behind the *Assembly* magazine, based in Kharkiv, Ukraine, have withstood the urge of nationalist militarism and chosen to focus on mutual aid, counter-information, and class conflict. All of the sections of the anarcho-syndicalist International Workers' Association (IWA) in the region – in Poland,[35] Slovakia,[36] Serbia,[37] and Russia[38] – have taken a clear stand for revolutionary internationalism. An 'Anti-militarist Initiative'

35. 'Against the War!', ZSP. https://zsp.net.pl/przeciw-wojnie. See also, anti-war actions in front of Russian and Ukrainian embassies. https://zsp.net.pl/anti-war-actions
36. Priama Akcia reproduced anti-militarist articles from CNT-AIT and KRAS.
37. 'Let's turn capitalist wars into a workers' revolution!', ASI. https://iwa-ait.org/content/lets-turn-capitalist-wars-workers-revolution
38. 'No War!', KRAS. https://aitrus.info/node/5921

based in Central Europe was launched in response to the surge of militarism across Europe, not least in the anarchist movement. They may be a minority, but anarchists have no faith in the inherent virtues of any majority. There is also a problem of Eurocentrism in the *East versus West* dichotomy, since internationalist reactions to the invasion of Ukraine can be seen from around the world.

Even without such concrete examples, we should be sceptical of anyone who claims to speak on behalf of a whole region, as if the anarchists of Eastern Europe were a homogenous collective with a consensus of opinion. The logic of representation itself must be scrutinised by anarchists. Those speaking for the region "extract only one tendency from the multidimensional whole and ignore or downplay the others".[39] In contrast "We try to listen to as many voices as possible, but we only support those that we find constructive. Others we criticize and refuse to support. In short, we perceive

---

39. 'Anarchist Antimilitarism and Myths About the War in Ukraine', Some Anarchists from the Central European Region.

different tendencies and do not try to support war propaganda that portrays the Ukrainian population as a united community calling unanimously for involvement in the war."[40] We should listen, yes, but also think for ourselves.

I totally reject the construction of an *us and them* paradigm between Eastern Europe and Western Europe. We relate to each other as individuals and collectives on the basis of shared struggles and shared principles, not as geopolitical blocs. KRAS (the Russian section of the IWA) have been slandered and had their members doxxed[41] for not falling into line behind the supposed pro-Ukraine "consensus", despite their anti-war efforts. One of the perpetrators of this doxxing was subsequently given a platform in Britain by *Freedom*,[42] in an interview about the defunct RKAS of Ukraine, an

---

40. *Ibid.*
41. 'Again about "anarchists" who forget the principles', KRAS. https://iwa-ait.org/content/again-about-anarchists-who-forget-principles
42. ' "Leftists" outside Ukraine are used to listening only to people from Moscow: Interview with anarcho-syndicalists in Eastern Ukraine', *Freedom*.

organisation accused of cult-ish authoritarian dynamics and nationalist sympathies, whose members dissolved into the conflict between the Ukrainian state and Donbass separatists.[43] At the same time, the editors of *Freedom* refused to publish anything contrary to their pro-Ukraine line.[44] This kind of tribalism can tear international movements apart.

Working Class Internationalism

> *"The position of 'no war but the class war' is not a cop-out, it is a long term and short term principle which denies the false choice between 'evils'. To make it a reality we need to be even more active in encouraging internationalism in the working class to the extent that ordinary people feel confident, organised and supported enough to resist their war-mongering governments and national liberation movements."*
>
> — *Organise! #52 (1999),*
> *Anarchist Federation*

---

43. 'Caution: platformist party and psychosect in one bottle!', Eretik. https://eretik-samizdat.blogspot.com/2013/01/caution-platformist-party-and.html
44. See, 'Fuck Leftist Westplaining', by Zosia Brom, *Freedom*.

Make no mistake, in opposing capitalist wars we are not pleading for peace at all costs. We are not pacifists. There can be no peace between people so long as one part of society oppresses and exploits the rest. The violent enforcement of power and wealth underlies everything in our society, and in times of war it erupts to the surface in a terrible orgy of blood. One power structure clashes with another; but whoever wins, our slavery continues. Our struggle is to overturn these powers and build new social forms without hierarchy. We will not be passive victims of violence: every struggle for freedom must defend itself when necessary. There is a long history of libertarian partisans fighting against oppressive governments and occupiers. Armed militias and guerilla units answerable to self-organised workers (such as revolutionary unions and workers' councils) have sprung up in times of social revolution.[45] *The people armed* are the surest safeguard

---

45. The formation of militias by the CNT-FAI in Spain, July 1936 – prior to their regularisation into the armed forces of the Republic – are a good example of this.

against counter-revolution. But regular armies – permanent, specialised forces monopolising legitimate violence with hierarchical discipline – are a function of state power (and a rudiment of the state-in-formation).[46]

In Ukraine and Russia there is no revolution, only war. The war between nations, then, must be transformed into open class struggle and rebellion against the war machine. This begins when workers reject the social truce within their "own" nation, and organise on a class basis against the people who oppress and exploit them every day.[47] Internationalists aim to build solidarity between workers across borders, while agitating for soldiers to fraternise, desert, and mutiny. Military infrastructure can be sabotaged, as has been happening on the railways connecting Russia and Belarus to

46. For example, the regularisation of the anarchist militias [see footnote above] into the military of the bourgeois-Stalinist Republic, alongside the disarming of CNT Defence Councils in the towns and cities, was a key stage of counter-revolution and reinforcement of state power in the Spanish Civil War.
47. See, for example, 'Wildcat strikes in Ukraine on both sides of the front line', *Assembly*.

Ukraine.[48] Mutual aid networks can be set up, so that people can support each other to survive the devastation and hardship.[49] Support needs to be given to draft-evaders, deserters, prisoners, and refugees.[50] All such vital efforts, and newly emerging forms of social struggle, should be organised from below, independent of all state, military, and corporate structures. Anarchists can take the initiative in agitating and organising such activity, while arguing for working class internationalism and opposing the authoritarian measures of the militarised state.

Workers around the world can intensify the latent struggle in their workplaces and

---

48. See, also, the fire-bombing of military recruitment offices across Russia, and the sabotage campaign of the 'Anarcho-Communist Combat Organisation' (BOAK).

49. The 'Solidarity Collectives' and *Assembly* have both been actively organising humanitarian aid for civilians.

50. Soldiers will be more likely to refuse to fight if they know there will be a support network to aid them when facing the consequences (or help to evade them). The prosecution and abuse of deserters and conscientious objectors has already begun. See, "Repression against those who do not want to fight", KRAS. https://aitrus.info/node/6044

communities, taking direct action against war industries and arms trading through strikes, boycotts, and sabotage. It is imperative that we oppose war-mongering and militarisation in Britain and Europe, resisting the generalisation of war. Direct action is already being used effectively by activists against arms companies linked to the Israel Defense Forces, for example.[51] We need to link the class struggle in Britain, which is currently growing in intensity due to the cost of living crisis, to the struggles faced by the working class in Ukraine and Russia. 'NWBCW Liverpool' have been agitating on this basis on picket lines across Merseyside during the current strike wave. We need to spread information about the daily struggles and emerging acts of rebellion in warring territories, and find ways to support them in practice.[52] Meanwhile we can seek to assist the people fleeing the war, whether they be civilian refugees or

51. Although I don't fully agree with their politics, 'Palestine Action' are a good example of the potential for direct action.
52. *Assembly*'s libcom blog is a good source of information on this subject. https://libcom.org/tags/assemblyorgua

military deserters.[53] The 'Olga Taratuta Solidarity Initiative' in France offers a good example of such practical support. This should bolster a broader struggle against the "Fortress Europe" border regime and Britain's "hostile environment" policy. Some anarchists in Britain have taken this course of working class internationalism – such as the Anarchist Communist Group, Liverpool Solidarity Federation,[54] and AnarCom Network – but they are a minority.

The Russian invasion of Ukraine and the immiseration of the working class in Britain are both products of the same capitalist system in crisis. And

---

53. The Anti-Militarist Initiative report that "At least 200,000 people are fleeing Russia to escape Putin's military mobilisation, and tens of thousands more are avoiding mobilisation in Ukraine. Yet some voices claim that *the number of deserters is so negligible that it is strange to even begin to talk about it.*' These cynical attempts to 'make invisible' people who choose not to serve in the army, to defect or to emigrate for political reasons, must be opposed. Their voices must be heard and practical help must be given." Quoting 'Appeal: Days of international solidarity with deserters'.

54. Liverpool SolFed set up 'No War But the Class War - Liverpool', alongside the Communist Workers' Organisation. https://nwbcwliverpool.wordpress.com/

this capitalist crisis can only be overcome by the revolutionary struggle of the international working class. If that *revolutionary* struggle and *international* working class solidarity have yet to develop, it is our task to help bring them about.[55] What was said by anarchists during the First World War is no less true today: "No matter where they may find themselves, the anarchists' role in the current tragedy is to carry on proclaiming that there is but one war of liberation: the one waged in every country by the oppressed against the oppressor, by the exploited against the exploiter. Our task is to summon the slaves to revolt against their masters."[56] Desertions, mutinies, mass strikes, and international revolutionary upheaval brought that war to an end.

---

55. Some anarchists have justified collaboration by arguing that the lack of a strong revolutionary movement in Russia or Ukraine makes an (internationalist) anarchist approach unworkable. But this logic would result in anarchists abandoning anarchism for the preferable faction of the ruling class every time circumstances push them to make this choice (i.e. every decisive historical moment). Anarchism would thus devolve into a liberal, reformist politics.
56. 'Anti-War Manifesto', February 1915, various authors.

In Britain we are at the heart of the global capitalist economy and NATO imperialism; to fall into war fever at this time is disastrous. The class struggle is already being waged by our bosses, bankers, oligarchs, and their lackeys in government: we can fight back or we can go to the slaughter.

Further Reading:

- 'War in Ukraine and desertion: Interview with the anarchist group "Assembly" of Kharkiv', International Relations Commission of the Italian Anarchist Federation.
- https://umanitanova.org/guerra-in-ucraina-e-diserzione-intervista-con-il-gruppo-anarchico-assembly-di-kharkiv-iten/
- 'An interview with anarchosyndicalists from Russia: no war but the class war!', Grupo Moiras.
- https://libcom.org/article/interview-anarchosyndicalists-russia-no-war-class-war
- 'Anarchist Antimilitarism and Myths About the War in Ukraine', Some Anarchists from the Central European Region.

- https://theanarchistlibrary.org/library/anony-mous-anarchist-antimilitarism-and-myths-about-the-war-in-ukraine
- Assembly coverage of anti-war direct action and social struggle in Ukraine and Russia.
- https://libcom.org/tags/assemblyorgua
- 'Against Nationalism', Anarchist Federation.
- https://theanarchistlibrary.org/library/anarchist-federation-against-nationalism